THE
DUST BOWL

A HISTORY PERSPECTIVES BOOK

Christine Zuchora-Walske

Published in the United States of America by Cherry Lake Publishing
Ann Arbor, Michigan
www.cherrylakepublishing.com

Consultants: Jason LaBau, PhD, U.S. History, Lecturer, California State
Polytechnic University, Pomona; Marla Conn, ReadAbility, Inc.
Editorial direction: Red Line Editorial
Book design and illustration: Sleeping Bear Press

Photo Credits: Arthur Rothstein/Library of Congress, cover (left), 1 (left),
4, 6, 11; AP Images, cover (right), 1 (right), 9, 14, 25; Dorothea Lange/
Library of Congress, cover (middle), 1 (middle), 16, 18, 30; Russell Lee/
Library of Congress, 22; Library of Congress, 26

Library of Congress Cataloging-in-Publication Data
Zuchora-Walske, Christine.
 The Dust Bowl / Christine Zuchora-Walske.
    pages cm. – (Perspectives library)
 Includes index.
  ISBN 978-1-62431-417-9 (hardcover) – ISBN 978-1-62431-493-3 (pbk.)
– ISBN 978-1-62431-455-1 (pdf) – ISBN 978-1-62431-531-2 (ebook)
1. Dust Bowl Era, 1931-1939–Juvenile literature. 2. Droughts–Great
Plains–History–20th century–Juvenile literature. 3. Farmers–
Oklahoma–History–20th century–Juvenile literature. 4. Migrant labor–
California–History–20th century–Juvenile literature. 5. Journalists–
California–History–20th century–Juvenile literature. I. Title.
F595.Z83 2014
973.917–dc23
                              2013006359

Cherry Lake Publishing would like to acknowledge the work of
The Partnership for 21st Century Skills. Please visit *www.p21.org*
for more information.

Printed in the United States of America
Corporate Graphics Inc.
July 2013
CLFA11

TABLE OF CONTENTS

In this book, you will read about the Dust Bowl from three perspectives. Each perspective is based on real things that happened to real people who lived during the Dust Bowl. As you'll see, the same event can look different depending on one's point of view.

CHAPTER 1..4
Vernon Thompson: Oklahoma Farmer

CHAPTER 2..14
Evelyn Brown: Migrant in California

CHAPTER 3..22
Florence Lee: Government Journalist

LOOK, LOOK AGAIN...................................30

GLOSSARY..31

LEARN MORE..31

INDEX...32

ABOUT THE AUTHOR...............................32

1

Vernon Thompson
Oklahoma Farmer

I was born in 1923 on a farm in Cimarron County, Oklahoma. That's in the Oklahoma **panhandle**. I've lived in Oklahoma all my life, and I've loved it all my life too. How could anybody not love its beautiful blue skies and wide-open grasslands?

For part of my childhood, though, Oklahoma was hideous. Every now and then, I still have a nightmare about a black blizzard, animal corpses, or my daddy crying. You see, I grew up during the Dust Bowl years of the 1930s. We called this time the "Dirty Thirties."

My family has been here since the 1880s. Back then just a handful of sheep and cattle ranchers lived here. My ancestors raised sheep. Few folks farmed back then—or at any rate, they didn't grow much. The prairie sod was really tough. It was hard to break up with a horse-drawn plow. And the weather was awfully dry too. A **drought** dragged on through much of the 1890s, when my momma and daddy were little.

But over time, more settlers arrived. The drought ended. Plows got bigger and better, and farmers started using motorized tractors. The ranches steadily turned into farms.

By the time I came along, people had plowed up the prairie. What had once been a vast, thick thatch

▲ *More and more farms were created on the Great Plains in the early 1900s.*

of grass was now an expanse of powdery **topsoil**. Cimarron County had become a paradise of fertile dirt and waving wheat, just like the rest of the southern Great Plains.

But in 1931, when I was eight, it stopped raining. At first no one worried much. Rain had fallen pretty regularly for 25 years before this. A lot of folks were new to Oklahoma. They came during these rainy years and figured it would always be rainy. They didn't know that in these parts, there's a normal cycle of rain and drought. So people kept on plowing and planting. But the rain didn't come.

When the first dust storm approached our farm in September 1931, we saw a wall of darkness in the distance. We thought it was a tornado. Momma told us to hightail it down into the root cellar.

As the storm blew over us, we could tell it was no tornado. They say a tornado sounds like a freight train. This storm sounded like a blizzard. The wind wailed overhead. It lashed the house with … something. We didn't know what.

Turns out it was dirt, not snow. After the wind stopped, Daddy pushed up on the cellar door with his shoulder. The door swung open, and bushels of

SECOND SOURCE

▶ Find another source on the September 1931 duster. Compare the information there to the information here.

black dust fell in. It billowed through the cellar, coating everybody with sooty powder.

As we climbed up and out of the cellar, we gaped at the farmyard. Black dust was everywhere. We walked up the porch steps, breaking a trail through the dirt. We opened the door and saw that the walls had been no match for the wind. Dust lay in a thick layer on every surface.

That was just the first of many dust storms. The next year we had 14, and the year after that, 38. There were 40 in 1935 and 61 in 1938. **Dusters** seemed to be blowing through here constantly.

I could tell where a duster had started by its color. Red meant it was Oklahoma dirt. Black dust came from Kansas. Gray came from Colorado and New Mexico. Dusters kept rolling over us like the wrath of God. But people had themselves to blame. They'd ignored the past and looked to the future with blinders on.

Farmers had torn up the plains to make money on wheat. While rain fell, wheat grew and the soil stayed put. But when the rain stopped, wheat wouldn't grow. Nothing held down the dry dirt, so the wind

▲ *Dust storms billowed over the plains, covering everything in their paths with a layer of dust.*

just carried it off. It gets mighty windy out here. There aren't many trees to slow down the air.

Throughout the 1930s, we lived in a fog of dust—indoors and out. No matter how often we washed, wiped, mopped, and swept, dust hung in the air and coated everything and everybody. We set the table under the tablecloth. We ate meals with our heads under the cloth. Dust sifted into our clothes, hair, and mouths. It ground between our teeth. We spat up clods of dirt.

Being dirty all the time was unpleasant, but it wasn't as bad as being hungry. At our house, it didn't happen often. A few times, though, we went to bed with empty stomachs. I didn't sleep well those nights. My gnawing innards and my parents' anxious voices kept me awake.

▲ *Farmers on the plains tried to save their crops that were buried in dust.*

The dust and heat killed lots of animals. People would find their livestock dead in the field or the barn. Sometimes animals starved or suffocated. Sometimes they ate too much dust. Butchering revealed stomachs coated with dirt two inches thick.

The dust sickened people too. You couldn't avoid breathing it. It settled into people's lungs and caused an infection called **dust pneumonia**. We didn't have any medicine for it, so lots of folks died.

They were a hard few years. Many people gave up and left for California. We hated to see our neighbors go, knowing we'd likely never hear from them again. But who could blame them? About three-quarters of us stayed put though. Some folks were too poor to go anywhere. Others simply refused to give up.

Folks got by any way they could. Those who lost their farms or businesses took odd jobs. We hung on to our farm. We found that turnips and potatoes were tough. We grew just enough to eat a little, sell a little, and hold down some topsoil. Daddy was a good hunter, and Momma was a clever penny-pincher. But it took all of us, working all the time, to survive.

STAYING PUT

Local newspaper editor John McCarty encouraged people to stay by forming the Last Man's Club. Its pledge: "In the absence of an act of God, serious family injury, or some other emergency, I pledge to stay here … and … help other last men remain in this country."

Evelyn Brown
Migrant in California

I was born in 1920. My family lived in Elkhart, Kansas. That's just north of the Oklahoma panhandle. My ma and pa ran a hardware store. In the 1920s, the local wheat farmers were making money hand over fist. They spent plenty of it at our store, buying tools and supplies and whatnot. So we did pretty well. We had indoor plumbing and electricity. Most of our neighbors didn't have either. We owned a pickup truck too.

Elkhart was small but busy. It had many shops and businesses, a school, and the Morton County courthouse. The hustle and bustle was exciting to grow up around. I felt lucky to live there.

By 1935, when I was 15, I felt a lot less lucky. A drought had dragged on for years. Dust storms raged constantly. Farms were failing. Many people left Morton County to try their luck elsewhere. Those who stayed were struggling to survive. Nobody could afford new stuff. Merchandise just sat in our store, gathering dust.

We scraped by for a while. But it was getting difficult to feed ourselves. We didn't have a potato patch, cows, chickens, or pigs, like

ANALYZE THIS

▶ Find another perspective that describes life on the Great Plains during the Dust Bowl. How is it similar to this perspective? How are the two different?

many folks did. We had to buy all our food. That was a tall order when there wasn't enough to go around.

There weren't any jobs either. So Ma and Pa decided we'd best get out of Elkhart while we still could. They'd heard California was a land of opportunity. They figured we could get a small farm plot there or at least find steady work. We piled our belongings in the truck bed and sold what wouldn't fit. We didn't make much money on the stuff we sold.

Then we drove south to stop at my uncle's house in Oklahoma. It was hard watching Pa bid his brother

Many plains families moved West in hopes of better lives. ▶

farewell. They didn't know if they'd ever meet again. We continued south into Texas, where we turned west onto Route 66. That two-lane highway would take us all the way to California, a journey of about 1,000 miles.

First we drove by day, crossing the Texas panhandle, New Mexico, and Arizona. We could cover about 200 miles between sunup and sundown. We stopped only to eat or to relieve ourselves. At night, we camped on the west side of billboards. In the morning, the billboards shaded us from the rising sun. When we reached the California border, we started driving by night. Ahead lay the Mojave Desert. It was dangerously hot in the daytime, so we had to cross it in the dark.

Finally we crossed the Tehachapi Mountains. After our long drive through the dry Southwest, the valley that spread out before us looked like the Promised Land. It was so green!

As we descended into the valley, we marveled at the vast fruit and vegetable fields. We headed for

Bakersfield, a big town at the southern end of the valley. We thought that was the best place to inquire about farmland and employment.

As we drove along, the scenes confused us. The fields were practically exploding with produce. But it didn't look as if this place was being kind to folks from the plains. Many of them lived in filthy, jumbled tent villages and **shantytowns** along the **irrigation ditches**.

Many migrants lived in makeshift homes, which were all they could afford. ▼

At first we didn't understand why people were so poor in such a rich land, but we soon figured it out. Thousands of **migrants** had come here looking for opportunity, but there was no land to be had. Huge, factory-style farms owned it all. The only work available was picking produce for these farms.

SECOND SOURCE

▶ Find another source on the conditions in migrant worker camps. Compare the information there to the information here.

Because so many pickers needed work, growers could pay whatever they liked. What they liked to pay was a trifle. People took the low pay because they had no other choice. They lived in squalor because they couldn't afford to do otherwise. They'd spent everything they had to get here.

We became part of the **refugee** group. Most of us weren't from Oklahoma, but the locals called us all Okies anyway. The locals sure didn't think much of us. Many of them wouldn't even talk to us.

Maybe they were afraid of us. We were desperately poor. We looked like something the cat dragged in. They thought we talked funny compared to them. There were so many of us, and we stuck around, unlike the Mexican migrant workers who seemed to come and go. I suppose the locals felt protective of their resources. It was the Great Depression, and times were bad all over.

It took us a long time to find a place to live. For a few months, we lived in our tent at the edge of an orange grove where we worked as pickers. We made only a penny per crate of fruit, so we all worked hard every day. Finally we scraped together enough cash and were able to rent a two-room cabin on the outskirts of Bakersfield.

Many migrant families moved around, following harvests. But Ma and Pa wanted to stay put so I could attend high school. Dust storms and traveling had disrupted my education, but Ma and Pa insisted that I get a diploma. They wanted me to have choices besides manual labor.

Ma found a job washing dishes at a diner. Her wages were low but steady. They helped even out Pa's unpredictable picking pay. I picked during summer break. I took a lot of insults at school for being an Okie and a picker, but I tried to keep my eyes on the prize. And little by little, things got better for us.

THE GRAPES OF WRATH

John Steinbeck's 1939 novel *The Grapes of Wrath* depicts the plight of Dust Bowl migrants through the story of the fictional Joad family. The Joads trek from Oklahoma to California, suffering scorn and hardship as they seek honest work. It is still widely read and discussed.

Florence Lee

Government Journalist

I was born in 1898 in Berkeley, California. My father was a professor of history at the university there. My upbringing was a little unusual. Back then, most girls set their sights on marriage. I set mine on my passion— photography. When I finished my studies at the New York Institute of Photography, I came back to California. I opened a portrait studio in San

Francisco. The 1920s were good to San Francisco, so I had plenty of business. Lots of rich and middle-class people wanted to capture themselves in photographs.

That all changed in 1929. Banks and businesses started failing left and right. Unemployment soared. My clients stopped coming. I didn't stop taking photos though. I just changed what I photographed.

I wanted to record what was happening in my city. So I started photographing the down-and-out of San Francisco. My subjects didn't pay me, of course, but I sold some of my work to newspapers. The sales were enough to cover my expenses if I lived very simply.

By 1935, I'd taken so many of these photos that people outside California started to notice. I got a letter from the U.S. Farm Security Administration (FSA). The FSA said the government needed professional photographers to document the plight of Great Plains residents and migrants. The photos would help Americans understand the problem of the Dust Bowl. They would also promote the

FSA's programs to help victims. Would I be interested in photographing those who'd moved to California?

Of course I would. This job was right up my alley. And I was glad for the offer of a steady paycheck. It was only four dollars per day, but that was enough. I loaded up my car and headed to the Imperial Valley in southeastern California.

As I entered the valley, I passed scenes unlike anything I'd photographed in San Francisco. Up to 6,000 migrants per month were coming to California—and it looked like most of them were coming here.

Migrant settlements were everywhere. I saw makeshift camps on the banks of irrigation ditches. I saw migrants using the ditch water for cooking and washing. I saw huge crowds at the relief offices. I saw whole families, including small

THINK ABOUT IT

► Determine the main point of this paragraph. Pick out one piece of evidence that supports it.

▲ *Many times all family members, including children, needed to work to earn enough money to survive.*

children carrying sacks twice their size, stooping in

the fields and picking peas under the blazing sun.

I tackled this job the same way I took newspaper

photographs in San Francisco. I tried not to stand out.

I lived alongside my subjects at the migrant camps.

We photographers had better food and beds and

▲ *FSA photographers captured images that showed the plight of migrant workers and people on the plains.*

so on, but it was rough living. I slipped into the community around the edges. I followed my hunches.

I figured I'd best be straightforward with my subjects. I would walk through the fields and talk to people, asking simple questions about what they were picking, how long they had been here, and when they ate lunch.

Then I'd say, "I'd like to photograph you." Most folks answered, "Sure, why not?" As time went on, folks got used to seeing me with my camera and paid me no mind.

Sometimes they would pose a little. When they posed, I would ignore them and walk about until they forgot me and went back to work. Then I'd start snapping photographs again.

Everybody was desperately poor, but I wasn't trying to show their poverty. I wanted to record qualities I saw in these people that were more important than their poverty. With my camera, I tried to capture their strength, spirit, pride, and courage. A few people wanted nothing to do with my photographs, but most folks understood I was trying to help them.

Some people called me a **propagandist**. They said I was

ANALYZE THIS

► Find another perspective that describes the life of migrant workers in California. How is it similar to this account? How is it different?

trying to shape public opinion with my photos. I think they meant to offend me, but I was not offended. I did want Americans to see what I saw. I knew that when they did, they would support efforts to care for the land and their fellow citizens.

I think we FSA photographers may indeed have helped a little. Partly in response to our work, the government started taking action. In 1937, the national government began building better camps for migrant workers. The new camps were clean and safe. They had bathrooms, showers, and gathering spaces. The California government joined in, offering child care, education, and medical programs. These changes gave migrants some measure of dignity, opportunity, community, and hope.

FSA photographers went to the Dust Bowl too. The images they captured there—of dust storms advancing on villages, automobiles buried in sand dunes, people groping their way through black blizzards, and more—helped Americans elsewhere identify with people on the plains. They fostered the understanding needed to pass soil **conservation** laws.

Soil conservation laws changed the way people farmed the Great Plains. Farmers began using practices that saved moisture and helped the soil stay put, such as planting trees and plowing along the contours of the land. These practices brought the plains back to life again.

PLAINS HELPER

Hugh Bennett was a scientist for the U.S. Department of Agriculture. He was one of the few people who recognized the danger of plowing up the prairie. In the 1920s, he predicted a disaster—and he was right. He wrote the soil conservation practices that eventually repaired the Great Plains.

LOOK, LOOK AGAIN

This is one of the most well-known images of the Dust Bowl. The image is often referred to as "Migrant Mother" and was taken by Dorothea Lange in 1936. The photograph shows a mother who was a poor migrant worker in California.

1. Imagine you are an Oklahoma farmer in the 1930s. What would you notice about this photograph?

2. Imagine you are a Dust Bowl refugee in California, like the woman in this picture. What would you be thinking about? How would you describe your living situation in a letter to your relatives on the East Coast?

3. Imagine you are a government journalist. Why would you take a photograph like this? In what ways does this photograph represent the Dust Bowl years?

GLOSSARY

conservation (kahn-sur-VAY-shuhn) the protection or preservation of valuable things

drought (DROUT) a long period without rain

dust pneumonia (DUST noo-MOHN-yuh) a sickness resulting from breathing large amounts of dust; symptoms include coughing, difficulty breathing, fever, nausea, and body aches

duster (DUS-tur) a windy dust storm

irrigation ditch (ir-uh-GAE-shuhn DICH) a ditch that carries water meant for crops

migrant (MYE-gruhnt) a person who moves from place to place in search of work

panhandle (PAN-han-duhl) a narrow area of land sticking out from a larger territory

propagandist (prah-puh-GAN-dist) someone who spreads ideas for a specific purpose

refugee (ref-yoo-JEE) someone who flees danger

shantytown (SHAN-tee-toun) a settlement of poor people living in makeshift dwellings; a slum

topsoil (TAHP-soil) fertile soil near the surface of the ground, where plants grow

LEARN MORE

Further Reading

Phelan, Matt. *The Storm in the Barn.* Somerville, MA: Candlewick, 2009.

Sandler, Martin W. *The Dust Bowl Through the Lens: How Photography Revealed and Helped Remedy a National Disaster.* New York: Walker & Co., 2009.

Sugarman, Dorothy Alexander. *The Great Depression: A Migrant Mother's Story.* Huntington Beach, CA: Teacher Created Materials, 2009.

Web Sites

The Dust Bowl
http://www.pbs.org/kenburns/dustbowl
This Web site offers Dust Bowl videos, photos, interviews, and an interactive feature that lets readers pretend they are in the Dust Bowl.

Surviving the Dust Bowl
http://www.pbs.org/wgbh/americanexperience/films/dustbowl
On this Web site, readers can watch the public television film *Surviving the Dust Bowl* and read articles and interviews about related events and people.

INDEX

animal, 5, 12, 15

Bennett, Hugh, 29

California, 12, 16, 17, 21, 22, 23, 24, 27, 28
conservation, 29

drought, 5, 7, 15
dust, 8, 10, 12, 15
dust storm, 7, 8, 15, 20, 28

farm, 4, 5, 7, 8, 12, 15, 16, 18, 19, 29
Farm Security Administration (FSA), 23, 24, 28
farmer, 5, 9, 14, 29

government, 23, 28
Grapes of Wrath, The, 21

infection, 12

migrant, 19, 20, 21, 23, 24, 25, 27, 28

Oklahoma, 4, 6, 8, 14, 16, 19, 21

photograph, 22, 23, 24, 25, 26, 27
photographer, 23, 25, 28

soil, 6, 9, 13, 29

ABOUT THE AUTHOR

Christine Zuchora-Walske has been writing and editing books and articles for children, parents, and teachers for more than 20 years. Her books include many titles for children and young adults on science, history, and current events. Christine lives in Minneapolis, Minnesota, with her husband and two children.